# TWENTY-FOUR CHRISTMAS STORIES

## THIS BOOK BELONGS TO

_____

# TWENTY-FOUR CHRISTMAS STORIES

DEBRA KAATZ

ILLUSTRATIONS
EMILY SKINNER

THE PETITE BERGERIE PRESS

# Twenty-four Christmas Stories

published by

**THE PETITE BERGERIE PRESS**

Les Horts, 30460, Soudorgues, France

& 27 Ondine Road, London, SE 15 4ED

10P on every book sold goes to children's charities

*Twenty-four Christmas Stories*

ISBN 0-9549166-3-8

Designed and typeset in Garamond by Debra Kaatz

Printed on Five Seasons recycled paper

by Cromwell Press  www.cromwellpress.co.uk

# CONTENTS

Winter is a time
For storytelling,
Each tale leading to another.
May these twenty-four stories
Light up the darkness
Like candles on the Christmas tree
Or stars in the night.

# LITTLE BEAR

There was cold sparkling snow outside the large cave. Inside Little Bear slept with his bright red hat to keep his ears warm. He was snuggled down into Mother Bear's arms with a sweet smile on his face. The Bears slept all through the long winter in their warm cave. Little Bear was dreaming that he was on an island of floating ice with his friend Ping the penguin. They were slapping fish out of the water. Slap, slap and a fish would bounce out of the water into their mouths. This little island floated on a calm sea. They drifted near the shore until they came to a place curving outwards. It caught the island like a kind and gentle hand.

Little Bear and Ping stepped onto the land and looked up the hill. There they saw a house made from blocks of ice. Little Bear gallumphed with his paws and Ping wiggle waggled on his penguin feet. The door to the ice house opened and out popped an elf. He was dressed in various shades of green with the longest stocking hat Little Bear had ever seen. It had a striped tassle at the end. With a chuckle the elf said, 'Come in, come in, the Jolly Toymaker loves a visit.'

As they walked through the door they saw a sparkling bright room with crystal walls. The elves, dressed in bright reds, blues, greens or yellows were making dolls, cars, computer games, balls and bats, puppets and wind-up toys. All the elves were laughing and singing making surprises for Christmas. Suddenly the Jolly Toymaker came towards them.

'Hello Ping and Little Bear. How do you like my workshop?' 'It's fun,' said Ping trying to play Catch the Starfish on a gameboy. Little Bear was trying to juggle with some brightly coloured bean bags. He could manage two but when he added the third one they all tumbled to the ground. Ping decided to try the racing cars. He raced them over bridges and mountains and then the doors became wings. They flew all over the room until they landed back on the floor. Little Bear went into the play cave where he found fairies and dragons. They danced together around the emerald green lake until they were out of breath and very dizzy.

Ping and Little Bear went into the next room where the elves were wrapping presents with coloured paper and sparkling ribbons. They had never seen so many boxes and parcels. Each one was for a very special boy or girl. 'Everyone is going to be so surprised on Christmas day,' laughed Little Bear.

In the next room cards were printed. One of the elves drew a picture of Ping and Little Bear and put it onto the printer. Out came name tags with their picture. They then watched as the elf tied the cards to presents and wrote children's names on them, carefully checking his long list. 'How can you remember everyone?' demanded Little Bear!

'With this,' laughed the Jolly Toymaker, holding up a magic wish-list crystal for recording the children's wishes and presents. The Jolly Toymaker then picked up two parcels wrapped in red paper with gold stars. His eyes were twinkling as he said, 'Now don't you two open these before Christmas!' 'Oh, no!' exclaimed Little Bear and Ping at the same time shaking their heads and crossing their hearts with their fingers.

Little Bear turned over at this point and opened his eyes in the cave and smiled. There lying next to him was the red package covered in stars just waiting for Christmas day. He sighed and smiled and then snuggled down to sleep. Who knows what his other dreams might bring.

# THE ROBIN

As the sun rose, the Robin puffed up his bright red feathers and cleared his throat to sing. Out came beautiful singing notes full of trills and vibratos. He began with a slow sweet song as the giant red sun rose out of the earth. He sang a fast jig as the insects whirled faster and faster in the air. The bees came out and his voice danced with them as they swarmed from flower to flower. He then flew off into the woods to find his breakfast of sleeping termites and juniper berries.

He was always alone in the winter. The tits and the sparrows flocked together. The jays and martins and owls flew in pairs. It was only the poor Robin that was on his own without the company of another robin.

However, the Robin had his songs. When he sang these songs they filled his heart with warmth and love. At dawn he sang his song about the wonderful rising sun. At the end of the day he did a quiet chant as the sun set. The Robin sang of the wonders of the stars and moon with a low voice. He made a laughing song as the squirrels flew from tree to tree. The Robin sang a sad song when a forest creature died and a joyful song when the spring eggs hatched into tiny birds.

One day, the Robin had an idea. He thought it would be wonderful if all the forest birds could learn his songs. These songs had been sung by Robins for hundreds of years. He went to the Owl. The Owl with his deep voice said, 'I would love to learn the Robin-songs to add to my Whoooooos.' He helped the Robin tell all the other birds. Soon all over the forest the birds heard the Owl calling out, 'Whoooooo will come to sing? Whooo will come to sing? Everyone come and sing this morning, whooooooooooooo.'

The jays, the martins, the owls, the tits and even the sparrows gathered together at sunrise. They tittered, whittered, chirped and cheeped, warming up their voices. The Robin tapped his wings together. There was a hush. The Robin started his Christmas song. He sang it right through to the end. Then he sang the first line again and they all repeated the line together. He did this line by line until the birds knew the whole song by heart. The owls sang the base notes, the jays hummed the full contralto notes, the sparrows tittered in soprano, the tits improvised, and the martins kept the melody. Finally they were ready to sing together. The Robin started with his solo followed by the full chorus.

The sun smiled on all the birds. All the animals stopped to listen to the most wonderful dawn chorus they had ever heard. Even the earth joined in with her gurgling streams and rustling leaves. The winds added some soft touches of oooooh and ahhhhh. The animals and plants and trees all clapped together. 'More, more,' they called out. The birds began to sing again with even more spirit. All the animals were soon dancing and the trees swaying. The sun began twirling in the sky. The insects by this time had learned the words and were busy buzzing along. The bears and the wolves tapped and banged to the rhythm and added a roar and howl to the magic of the morning. Everyone was joining in and all the forest was alive with the special song.

The Robin was no longer alone. All around him were a hundred voices singing his special Christmas song. His cheeks were as bright as his red feathers and his heart was full of joy. They had enjoyed it so much that each day after that, until Christmas, everyone came together to sing a new Christmas song.

# THE SNOW QUEEN

Deep amongst the white snow clouds in the sky is a castle made of blue ice. Here the Snow Queen, with her long white hair, and flowing robes covered in snowflakes, stood watching the sky. Her crystal blue eyes looked at the silver moon as she waited for the snow. When the first flakes fell, she left the window and flew down the stairs to her crystal chariot in the courtyard. She took up the reins of her four white horses whose breaths were pouring white smoke into the frosty air. Slowly they climbed into the sky until they were over the city, where large flakes of snow were dusting the roofs and streets.

She laughed like the ringing of a crystal bell. She saw her friend the North Wind coming across the sky. He smiled and said in his very deep voice, 'Shall we dance and make snow together?' The Snow Queen blushed and giggled and said, 'Yes, let's begin with a waltz.' She threw blue crystals in the air to make more snow, as her chariot raced into the sky. She and the North Wind danced and whirled. The snow swirled everywhere until the earth was covered in soft white powder. The world itself grew quieter and quieter.

Animals dug themselves deep into the snow and went to sleep in little hollows protected from the wind. The trees were covered in large white coats and looked like giant frozen statues with spindly arms and long fingers. The mountains were covered in white blankets. They looked like a giant white sea serpent with its head buried in the snow. The houses had white frosting for roofs and lacy patterns on the windows. Ice crystal sculptures of strange beasts formed in the streams and rivers. The lake was frozen into a giant mirror. Even the moon had become a silver coin covered in a white veil.

The Snow Queen flew to the moon and watched as the world became a kingdom of soft white crystals. She wanted it to have more details. So the North Wind blew even harder and the Snow Queen's chariot danced on the waves making great drifts and patterns in the snow. All night long the Snow Queen and the

North Wind danced. Together they covered the landscape in layers and layers of soft cold whiteness until everything was still and soft.

As the children woke that morning their faces were full of wonder and delight. They looked at the mountain serpent with its head in the snow and watched as the trees dropped bits of white clothing on the ground. There were bird prints in the snow and cat trails. The squirrels sent the snow flying as they poked their heads out to see what had happened while munching their nuts. The roads had disappeared and the postman came along wearing snow shoes carrying Christmas letters and parcels in a sack on his back. He was whistling with rosy cheeks.

The children took out tracing paper and put it on the windows. They then set to work copying the patterns of the frost. Soon their paper was filled with beautiful snow crystals. They looked outside again and smiled for their world had become as wonderful as the snow palace of the Snow Queen. They dressed quickly and were soon playing in the wonderful whiteness.

High up in the clouds the Snow Queen and the North Wind sat in the ice castle drinking hot chocolate and eating sugar buns. They were hungry having worked all night making the snow. They smiled down on the world they had transformed into a winter wonderland and watched as the children came out to play.

# THE SNOWMEN

The snow had come with its soft slippers in the night never making a sound. Silently it had covered the world with a white fluffy blanket. There was no school as the roads were filled with snow and the children could play all day. The children gathered in the large field bundled up in boots, coats and warm woolly hats. They began rolling snow into tummies and then chests and finally heads. They gathered stones for eyes and holly for mouths with some berries for noses. They twisted ivy together for scarves and found twigs for arms. Pine branches made furry hats and chestnuts made buttons for snowy coats. Soon there were six snowmen watching the children slipping, sliding, rolling and tumbling in the snow.

The children sledded on the hill below. They used old chair legs with wooden slates on the top, plastic sacks, or dust bin lids to slide down the hill. They laughed and tumbled down the hill and then pulled their sleds up the hill to start all over again. The smaller children rested by the snowmen watching their brothers and sisters play on the hillside. The snowmen themselves seemed to laugh as they watched everyone roll and tumble in the soft powder.

One of the little girls made a feast for the snow men of snow cakes and snow tea and even snow sandwiches filled with leaves. Two of the youngest children made a snow bunny rabbit and then a snow dog chasing a snow cat. Finally the sun descended in the sky and the children waved goodbye to the snowmen. They went home to hot chocolate, sandwiches and cakes for tea.

That night as the clouds cleared, the moon and the stars shone their light on the Snowmen. The children were fast asleep dreaming of Christmas and all the presents that would be under the tree. The great owl in the old oak tree woke up and blinked his eyes. There on the snowy field he saw the Snowmen begin to move. They raised their arms to the moon in salute like snow soldiers. They began to dance in a slow heavy sort of way. It was as though they were learning to walk for the first time. They then put skis on their feet and slid up and down the hill. The snow dog and the cat jumped on a piece of wood and sledded down the hill as the children had done in the day.

The great owl flew in and out of the Snowmen. The wind whistled a dance tune and the badgers wagged their tails in time. Suddenly the snowmen began to dance a fast jig holding hands. The red foxes joined in, weaving in and out of the line the Snowmen had formed. They were howling a tune to the moon at the same time. This woke up the squirrels who brought nuts in a wooden bowl to pass around when the dancers had finished. The birds brought juniper berries and acorns. Soon everyone in the forest was dancing, drinking and eating by the light of the moon and stars.

As the moon began to go down in the west, the south wind began to blow with a warm breath. The Snowmen began to melt, growing smaller and smaller as they walked up the hill more and more slowly. At last they reached the place where they had been born. They stood there under the stars becoming even smaller until finally they disappeared. In the morning when the children awoke they saw only a small pile of snow in each place where there had been a snowman. They sighed but then remembered the fun they had and waved goodbye to the snow and the snowmen they had created.

# THE LAMP

A very, very, very long time ago, even before your great, great, great grandfather lived there was a not very nice king. He was never happy no matter how much he had. He keep the harvest and golden coins for himself and gave his people very little to eat. He would make them work hard and when they fell ill he would leave them to die. It was winter time and everyone was cold and hungry. They were so fed up with the King that some brave men met together one night and decided to fight and put an end to the King. They gathered stones and sticks and made shields of wood. They fought for many days. Sometimes they had to hide in the forest and wait. Then they would surprise the king's soldiers with rocks and stones. Finally one night three of the men quietly climbed into the great palace. They killed the King in his sleep. Everyone was happy especially the soldiers because they could rejoin their families.

The country was at last at peace but everywhere was in ruins. There were very few houses with roofs and the animals were scattered. It was winter and very cold and snowy. Everyone was dressed in rags. The soldiers led the men to the palace storehouse. There they found grain to make bread and material to make coats.

The old soldiers helped the men rebuild houses and shared out the food from the great palace storehouses. They gathered up straw and blankets so the children could sleep together in one large room. In the cellar below they put the animals who helped to keep the room warm. The women laughed and cooked together. The old women knitted and made warm clothes. An old cobbler made good sturdy boots for the men. The men repaired the city, cut wood and herded the animals.

Finally, it was time to repair the great temple the King had destroyed. In the temple the eternal light had burned every day and night without going out. The King had put out this light. He had also destroyed the oil for lighting the lamp because he did not want the people to believe in anyone but himself.

While the lamp burned the people could feel the love of the great spirit near to them. For this reason the people had kept the light going all the time to remind themselves that there was something greater than man. This great spirit helped and loved the world. When the temple was repaired they needed oil for the lamp but could not find any. They searched everywhere in the palace without success.

Then one little boy called out. He had found some oil in a corner of the old temple in an old blue bottle. It was just enough to light the lamp for one day. It would take eight days to make new oil. They lit the lamp, hoping. The next day it was still alight. They thanked the great spirit. The next day it was still burning and the people thanked the spirit again. It stayed alight for eight days until the new oil was ready. It was a miracle sent by the great spirit above to thank them for remembering him. They never forgot the miracle.

Each year after that in the middle of winter the people would gather food and make little presents for each of the children to celebrate this great miracle of the lamp. Even to this day people have continued to light candles for eight nights to remember how this one light lasted in those ancient times. They share food and give small gifts. As they light the candles the great spirit above shines down filling them with kindness and love that brings hope in the long winter.

# GINNY

Beatrice had a guinea pig named Ginny. Ginny lived in a cage with a rabbit named Snowy. Both Snowy and Ginny loved each other. They shared their cage in the garden where they could smell the flowers and the rain and the snow and all the animals that wandered past. Ginny was soft with white and brown fur and Snowy was all white like a furry snow ball. Often they would curl up together with their noses still twitching enjoying the smells all around them.

Beatrice came every morning to feed them before going to school. She gave them a mixture of rabbit cereal and some raw vegetables. One morning she put in some cabbage leaves. She watched as Snowy started munching one end of a leaf at the same time as Ginny nibbled the other end. As they reached the middle they touched noses and ate a final bite each. She gave them another big leaf and they did the same thing. She laughed and said, 'You two have a good day while I am working hard at school.'

Ginny looked at Snowy and asked, 'What is school?' 'Ah,' thought Snowy who had been taken there once on pets' day, 'there is a large room with lots of children and a teacher who asks them questions. They write things down on paper. When I was there they drew pictures of me. Some of them were quite good. They have their lunch and afterwards go out to play games. They then come back in and the teacher tells them a story.' 'I think I prefer to be out in the garden,' said Ginny.

When Beatrice came home in the evening, the weather was cold and cloudy but not yet snowing. She took both Ginny and Snowy out for a romp in the garden. She watched as they ate the grass and sniffed around. Sometimes Ginny would climb on Snowy's back and go for a ride. Then Snowy would tumble over. They both would turn on their backs and wiggle and jiggle and finally bounce back on their feet. 'You two could be circus clowns,' giggled Beatrice. When they had finally snuggled together again, Beatrice put them back into their cage and gave them their supper. They curled up in the hay together and watched the stars come out.

'What is a circus?' asked Ginny. Snowy thought and said, 'A circus is where there are big elephants and tigers and men that walk on a string high in the air.' 'I think the squirrels would be good at that,' smiled Ginny.

As Christmas approached Ginny was looking rounder and rounder. She seemed to eat and eat and eat. Beatrice looked at her and thought she looked sweet with a plump little belly. She thought that Ginny was probably just eating more because of the cold. She was definitely furrier with her thick winter coat.

That night Beatrice gave them some broccoli for a treat and

went inside to put her stocking up for Christmas eve. 'I will have a special treat for you tomorrow as it will be Christmas,' smiled Beatrice. 'What is Christmas?' asked Ginny. 'Well it is when the family has a tree and they give each other things wrapped in paper. They even wear funny hats at dinner,' said Snowy. 'It's to celebrate the birth of a boy prophet a long time ago.'

The following morning Beatrice came out to give them their breakfast. This included some cranberries as a Christmas treat. Beatrice looked into the cage and laughed in surprise. Ginny had three tiny babies lying next to her all suckling away. They were round and furry with pink noses. Beatrice named them Holly, Christmas and Ivy.

# YEW TREE

In the very centre of the forest lived an ancient Yew tree. It had watched the forest grow over hundreds of years. It knew all the animals that came to shelter under the trees, the deer, foxes and wolves as well as the birds, squirrels and moles. On this night its branches were covered in thick snow for it was the coldest and longest night of the year. The Yew was asleep with its life sap deep in its roots waiting for the spring.

Each year on this special night, when the sun would begin to come closer to the earth again, the Yew dreamed of the sun. It could feel that something was returning that would bring everything to life. It was a small movement in the stillness of the night. It woke the Yew who looked around at the calm, quiet forest in moonlight. Ah, yes, it remembered, the men would come this night.

It watched as the wizard and the men dressed in furs came through the forest with torches of light, singing and dancing. They built a bonfire near the Yew and sang to the stars and the great spirits above, asking them to bring a good New Year. The Yew smiled for it had already felt the change in its roots and knew the sun was coming back to bring the warmer days.

Many years ago the men had built a stone circle. First their wizard watched the night sky for a month carefully marking places in the direction of the stars. He then watched the sunrise on the shortest day of the year or the solstice. He had the men gather twenty-four large stones and place them upright in the deep holes he had dug. Over two of the stones he placed another stone so it was like a gateway to the stars. In the centre he placed three more stones. All through the years this stone circle gathered the energy of the sun, moon and stars bringing great goodness to the earth.

The stone circle was near the bonfire. After the men feasted on roasted meat and hot wines, they waited for the sun. As it rose out of the darkness it spread its light through the stone gateway. Everyone began to sing and dance to welcome its return. The light filled all of the stone circle.

The sunlight flowed through the stone archway into the centre of the stone circle lighting up the entire ring of stones. It was as though the whole world had been rekindled with the fire of the sunlight. The men thanked the sun and the Yew tree and asked them to protect the village and the crops for the next year.

The Yew rustled its branches and gathered the earth spirit in its roots to receive the special sunlight that had gathered in the circle. Through the great tree, the spirits of heaven and earth united to bring energy to the seasons. In this way there would come the rains and sunshine that would give good crops and keep away illness for the next year.

The Yew smiled to himself knowing all would be well and

with a sigh went back to sleep dreaming. The wizard felt the warmth return to the earth and bent down and thanked the great spirits. The men left offerings of food and wine by the tree and coloured ribbons in the centre of the circle. They left quietly knowing all would be well.

The Yew dreamt of the great chariot that carried the sun across the sky and the earth spirits that breathed life into each seed in the spring. He dreamt of the Greenman of forest. The Greenman whispered in the Yew's ear, that in spring he would come and wake all the trees and flowers and open the Yew tree's buds once again with fresh green leaves. The Yew sighed contentedly in his sleep.

# THE WIZARD'S CHRISTMAS PRESENT

It was not always easy to have a Dad who was a Wizard. There was the morning when he was changing the colour of the curtains in the living room for my Mum and changed my hair to bright red as well. I hadn't noticed until I got to school and wondered why everyone was looking at me. It was a good red colour not carrot colour like most red hair, but a bit of a surprise to my teachers. Fortunately it faded after lunch time when I had normal dull brown hair again.

Then there was the time he was shrinking a Giant who had come down the bean stalk in the garden. My sister got in the way and she shrunk to the size of a mouse. It took a week for that spell to wear off and she stayed in my shirt pocket so as not to miss school but to be safe from being stepped on. Ever since then she has had a passion for nuts.

One day he was working with a disappearing charm. My mother opened the door and bang! She became invisible. She had a lot of fun for two days suddenly speaking to us out of the air. I had to go with her shopping so it would look as if I was carrying the bags. Sometimes she would forget to whisper and I would have to explain I was practicing for the school play trying out different voices.

This year I was trying to think of a present for my Dad.

I wanted it to be a real surprise and special but I couldn't think of anything. So in the end I wrote to Father Christmas. I thought he, out of everyone, would know about presents, as he gave them to hundreds of people. I explained to him that my Dad was a Wizard. It was a week later when the reply came.

Father Christmas wrote and suggested that my Dad might like a flying machine. Wow, I thought to myself, that was a really good idea. So I set to work with my bits of wood and glue and created a time-flier. It had a gear-stick that moved it forward into the future and backward into the past. It was a model that could be carried in a pocket until it was needed. I painted it a bright red and gave it golden stripes along its wings. The seats had soft velvet cushions.

Christmas day arrived and the look on my Dad's face as he opened the present was wonderful. He was fascinated with the new toy and the little gears and levers. He liked the red colour. Then with his magic wand he created two flying scarves and hats. After lunch of turkey and Christmas pudding we went out into the garden. With an abrakadoo the flying machine became man-size.

We spent the afternoon going from one Christmas to another. We visited the Christmas when my grandparents were children. They had real candles on the tree and there were little sugar mice for each of the children. In their stockings were bright new pennies and wooden toys. We went into the future. The trees were made of holograms with whirling lights. The stockings were full of tiny recorders and films. We even went back to the time when Father Christmas was a boy. He was in his room doing the most amazing drawings of toys of the future. I never realized what a job it was to keep up with all the new toys.

It was finally time for tea. My Dad was suddenly hungry for the fruit cake he had as a boy. So we went to visit his family and they gave us a cake to take back. When we arrived home my Dad made the time-flier small again and put it on his magic things shelf until he would need it again. Together we ate the fifty year old Christmas cake.

# THE
# ORPHANAGE

The orphanage was a grey place. The blankets were grey, the walls were grey, the tiles were shades of grey and the Matron wore grey. It was a very, clean and orderly place, but so orderly nothing ever seemed to change. The twelve children who lived there were fed and dressed in grey and went to school and played quietly with each other. But finally something happened. The Matron fell over into her soup at lunch two days before Christmas. She was suddenly very dead. The Cook called the Doctor. He came and said she was dead and took her away to be buried underneath the cold snow. The Cook looked after the children for the day. They were even quieter than before.

The next morning it was snowing but the sky seemed blue and pink, not grey at all. As the children woke they heard sweet chimes and sleigh bells. There at breakfast was the new Matron. She was young, and pretty and wore coloured stockings and colourful dresses and smiled. There was hot chocolate and pancakes for breakfast with jams and honey in honeycombs. The Cook was singing Christmas songs.

After breakfast the new Matron lined up the children and changed their grey clothes, with a wink of her eye, into bright colours. Afterwards they cleared the tables. Out of a new giant cupboard appeared papers, glue, scissors, stickers, glitter and ribbons for making decorations. The grey walls were soon hidden away beneath the colours. The children were no longer quiet but laughing, talking, joking and really enjoying themselves.

Suddenly it was lunch time. They ate roast potatoes, golden brown crisp chicken and jam tarts in star shapes with golden custard. After that it was time for a walk. The children put on their newly coloured hats and coats and went out into the snow to the forest. They were going to get a real tree.

Never in all the years of the orphanage had they had a real tree for Christmas. They walked and slid on the snow. The smell of the air was cold and fresh. The trees sparkled with the new snow.

They passed a waterfall that had formed hundreds of giant ice crystals and looked like a fairy palace. Finally they came to a fir tree that was just the right size. The Matron smiled at the tree and asked, 'Could you spare the time to be our Christmas tree?' It laughed and bounced out of the ground. It said, 'My name is Teri the tree and I would love to be your Christmas tree. Will you decorate me with candles and put presents under my roots?' 'Yes, yes,' said all the children. 'Will you give me a present too?' asked the tree. The littlest child said, 'We will sing you Christmas songs.' 'Well,' smiled Teri the tree, 'I would like that and some nice earth and water.' So all the children shook hands with Teri the tree and it was a deal. Teri the tree walked home with them carrying the three smallest children in its branches.

They found a pot for Teri and filled it with nice soil so Teri would feel at home. They then made Teri into the most wonderful Christmas tree with an angel at the top. The Matron with another wink filled the branches with lighted candles and stars. The children's faces lit up in wonder. They decided to sing the song about the Christmas tree and Teri sang as well. They then softly sang Silent Night. The door opened and Cook came in with a tray full of cakes and sandwiches and hot chocolate. When they were all warm and full and sleepy the Matron told them the story of the angels.

# ANGELS

Angels have the job of looking after the wishes of the world and helping wherever they can. It is a big job so there are many different kinds of angels living in the great castle of clouds deep in the sky. Angelic was a tiny angel the size of a flower fairy. She listened to the dreams of children and did what she could to make them happy. She helped their wishes to come true. Sometimes this was just whispering ideas into their parent's ears. But sometimes it took more than that to change things so the children could laugh and play again.

Her brother Arche was the biggest angel ever. Arche was called on to fill the sky with light in the middle of battle fields. He would sometimes charge forth on giant horses to frighten the enemy and save the soldiers. He did things in a big way. One time he parted a great river and held the water each side so people could walk across out of danger. Another time he became a burning tree and handed down stone tablets with mighty words written on them. He could shake the earth with his hand and stir up the winds with his breath. What he really enjoyed was coming to earth as a brilliant angel of light. He would light the sky with hundreds of colours. Lightening and thunder would roll across the heavens as he created a miracle. Arche liked doing things in a dramatic way with as much light and colour as he could manage.

Angelic did things in a more individual way. They were more day to day miracles. Sometimes she would move cars out of the way so mothers could get to school on time. At other times she would trip up a school bully so he fell on his face instead of hitting a small child. Sometimes she made trees and flowers blossom. People would then smile and slow down and enjoy the beauty all around them.

Today the two angels were working together. It was two days before Christmas and many poor children in New York were still without presents. It was going to be close, but God had given them the job of seeing that no child was without a special gift. He wanted every child to have a present on Christmas day.

Angelic flew around listening to the children's hopes and dreams making a giant list of names and addresses and ideas for gifts. Often the children only wanted small things like a Christmas tree or a red skirt or some music or a racing car.

Arche dressed in his best light and appeared before the Mayor. He showed the Mayor all the poor houses and children in a series of visions. He then presented the list and left in a great flash of light. The Mayor was impressed and got to work on his twelve phones. He called his workers, the stores and the postmen. He gave his six secretaries the lists. Everyone stared working. They called in their families to help. The postmen worked late into the night. The chocolate factory made special chocolates for everyone on the list with a box for each family. This took extra time but it was such a wonderful idea no one minded the extra work. The Mayor and everyone helping him were full of the warmth and joy of giving.

Although it seemed to be a close thing, the night before Christmas, every name on the list had been crossed off and a present delivered. The Mayor gave each of the workers a box of chocolates and some sparkling wine. Arche and Angelic, looking down from heaven, smiled, thinking of the surprises and happy grins the morning would bring. They then opened their big box of chocolates. Angelic had a soft toffy and Arche had a supernova.

# BILLY

Billy lived with his Gran. His parents had died when he was born and she had looked after him ever since. They managed together. His Gran knitted for people. She made lovely patterned jumpers and warm woolly hats. Billy had jobs doing other people's gardens and did his paper round each morning. He was good at school because his Gran had taught him to read when he was very young. Gran had not been well for several months and the Doctor did not give her much hope. She still managed her knitting but was slower and slower getting up and down. Billy looked after her and made sure she was warm, well fed and had cups of tea.

That evening when they were having a cup of tea together, Gran said, 'Billy I have written to my son Ralph about you. He lives in Canada but I hope he will look after you when I am gone.' 'Oh, Gran, don't talk like that, you will outlast me.' 'No, Billy, the doctor knows about these things and he said I probably will not last until Christmas.' 'Oh, Gran, I love you,' said Billy tucking her up in bed. 'I love you too Billy, and always remember that. Remember too, that even if I am not here I will still look after you.' Billy read some of his book to Gran until she fell asleep. He watched her struggle to breathe for a while before going to bed.

The next morning Gran did not wake up. Billy sat by her bed a long time. Finally he called the doctor. 'Doctor Little, can you come quickly as Gran is no longer breathing,' said Billy quietly. 'I'll be there in a few minutes,' softly said the Doctor. Billy wanted his Gran so much it hurt everywhere inside, but he also knew she was somewhere in heaven near the God she always talked about. 'Oh God,' prayed Billy, 'please look after her.'

The doorbell went and Billy opened the door and saw a strange man outside. The man smiled and said, 'You must be Billy, is your Gran around?' Billy tried to swallow the knot in his throat and burst into tears, 'No, I mean, yes, but she's, well, she died in the night. I think she's with the angels she always talked about.' The man put his arm around Billy and said, 'I'm her son Ralph from Canada, I came as soon as I could.' The Doctor arrived next with the ambulance. They put Gran on a stretcher and Billy gave her a kiss and said a final goodbye. 'I hope the angels look after her.' 'I'm sure they will,' said Ralph.

There were many people at the funeral. Many of them wearing the beautiful jumpers Billy's Gran had knitted. They all came back to the house afterwards and Billy helped serve tea and Gran's favourite cakes. Somehow he felt she would approve.

After the funeral, Ralph and Billy went on a large plane to Canada. It was the day before Christmas. Billy loved looking down at the small houses and the tiny boats on the ocean. When they arrived in the airport, Billy met Ralph's two children, Jilly and Tom, his wife Sue, the dog, the cat and the three goldfish. Jilly said, 'I thought you would like to meet the pets too.' Billy smiled shyly and said, 'Thank you all for meeting me.' The dog, Toby, licked his hand. In the car the children talked and become the best of friends.

That night Billy hung up his stocking next to Jilly's and Tom's. It was a red and white striped stocking his Gran had knitted. On Christmas morning, there was a shiny new red bike for Billy. 'Wow,' exclaimed Billy, 'thank you so much.' The three children went riding bikes together through the snowy road. As Billy looked up into the sky he could see his Gran smiling down at them.

# THE UNICORN

Unicorns are rare. They live in the wild places deep in the forests, high in the mountains hidden by the clouds. Sometimes they can be seen flying across the sky on a night when there is a full moon. Living high in the mountains they can see great distances. Sometimes if you are very quiet you can sense there is a unicorn looking down at you. There are even times when certain unicorns decide to show themselves to a special child.

Stephen lived in a large city but always dreamed that one day he would meet a unicorn. When he was seven his Dad took him up into the mountains a few days before Christmas. At the top of the mountain the snow stayed all year around. As they walked through the valley they passed beaver dams and watched the beavers swimming in their pond. They saw deer from a distance and also a snake sunning itself on a rock. They walked higher and higher until they were above where the trees could grow. Here above the trees there were only the eagles that flew high in the air and the tiny alpine plants.

Stephen thought he could feel something watching him. He looked high up into the mountains but could only see the eagle flying overhead. He helped his Dad put up their tent for the night. He then gathered old bits of bushes and twigs. He made a circle of rocks and placed the wood in the middle and lit the fire. His dad cooked the sausages and potatoes on a stick and the baked beans in their tin. They ate their supper near the fire under the stars. When they had finished they had a chocolate bar and a cup of tea. Stephen crawled into his sleeping bag and was soon fast asleep.

In the middle of the night Stephen woke with a start. He thought he could hear something calling on the winds. He was very careful to climb out of his sleeping bag so he would not wake his Dad. He slipped out of the tent and was amazed at how light it was with the full moon.

He turned and there standing behind him was a Unicorn. The Unicorn was pure white with bright blue eyes. Slowly and gently Stephen came up to the Unicorn and stroked its neck.

'What are you called?' asked Stephen. 'Orion,' smiled the Unicorn, 'it is the star I come from. Over there to the left is the star constellation in the sky.' 'You are so beautiful,' said Stephen. 'Come,' said Orion, 'you can ride on my back.' Up they flew into the sky looking down on all the mountains under the large silver moon and bright stars. They flew over the city where Stephen lived and he said, 'You are the best Christmas present ever.' They circled around and returned to the mountains.

'Because you wished for me, I have come to see you,' said Orion. 'If you need help at any time you must call on me.' 'What kind of help?' asked Stephen. 'Oh, monsters, bad wizards, bullies or trolls.' 'Wow,' said Stephen,

'You mean I might meet those as well?' 'Yes, you might meet those as well and together we will defeat them!' When they came down to earth again, near the tent, Orion said, 'Take three hair from my mane. When you want to call on me whisper to the hairs and I will come.' Stephen took the three hairs and watched as the Unicorn disappeared into the snow.

When Stephen wanted to see the stars again or had to deal with monsters, he would whisper to the three hairs. Then the Unicorn would fly through his window and they would once again ride on the winds high above the beautiful mountains. They had many adventures together making the earth safe from monsters.

# CHRISTMAS PUDDING

The sky was bright blue and it was warm enough to fry an egg on the pavement. Christmas comes during the heat of the summer in Australia. In order to cool off we were going to the beach for the Christmas weekend. Dad tied the surfboards to the roof of our old car. We three kids sat in the middle seat and Bruno our soppy dog and Matilde the cat were in the back between the boxes of food. We sang Christmas songs through the open windows every time the car stopped. The people in the cars along side us joined in until we started off again. We finally got to the beach where there was bright sunshine on the silver sand. The sea stretched for miles and was as blue as the sky.

We found starfish and shells in the sandy beach as we went down to the ocean. We put our surfboards in the water and were soon out in the sea. We paddled out to the white crests and then stood up on our surfboards.

The joy of getting up on a wave and riding up and down and into another wave was wonderful. We stretched out our arms and flew. Then with a bump we would fall off the board and into the water. The coolness was fresh and tingled the skin. We grabbed the board and up we would go again finding one wave after another. There is nothing like surfing for building up an appetite for lunch. When Dad finally called, we were hungry.

Christmas Pudding

Dad had put the table under
the shade of the palm trees.
Mum put on the red cloth with
holly berries embroidered along
the edge. She set out the best
plates and glasses. She had made
everyone a red Christmas cracker
with their names on the outside.
Inside there were hats and jokes
and toys. We put on our shorts
and T-shirts and dusted the sand
off our feet.

We found our places and sat
down. Dad poured lemonade for
us and wine for him and Mum.
We toasted to each other and the
Queen and pulled the crackers
and put on the hats. We read
the jokes and saved the wind-up
cars to race later when Mum and
Dad took their naps. The turkey
pieces had been barbecued and
were served with salad and baked

83

potatoes. We dug in and finished everything in no time at all.

We paused before the desert while Dad turned on the car radio. We listened to the Queen's speech. The President of Australia then talked about having peace in the world. I thought to myself it would be good if everywhere there was peace for Christmas with every one enjoying good food. We toasted to the health of the world and waited for the Christmas songs to come on. We all joined in and the waves of the sea swished in time. Then Mum disappeared into the house. There was a great hush for we all knew the pudding was coming. Out she came holding the Christmas pudding in brandy flames. We sang We Wish You a Merry Christmas. When we got to the verse about wanting our figgy pudding we sang as loud as we could. We each had a slice with cream and brandy butter.

Dad went into the house to get the box of presents. He shout out everyone's name as he handed each of us our wrapped surprises. We opened our presents one at a time and oohhed and aahhed at what we each had been given. We thanked each other with kisses and hugs. Finally it was time to clear the table. Mum and Dad had put up hammocks under the trees and went off to take forty winks. We played with our cars on a piece of driftwood having all kinds of competitions while the adults slept. The sea waves were bright blue. Christmas under the sun was just as much fun as Christmas in the snow.

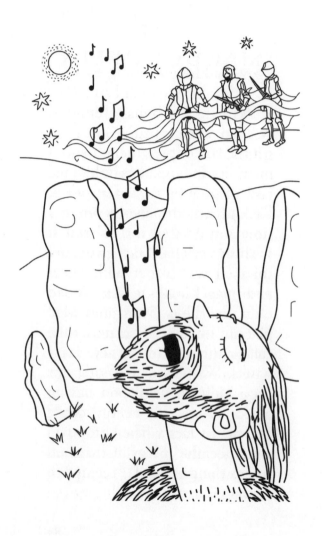

# THE
# MACDOUGELLS

Outside the village there is an ancient circle of large stones, twice the height of a man. Each week I would take Jake my dog up there for a walk. I could feel the energy when I stood inside the ring of stones. It always gave me tickles up my spine. It was like standing next to an angel or being surrounded by stars. The twelve stones were placed there by sacred men called the Druids. They must have known about the earth for they built the stone circles in places where this energy could be felt. In fact when I stood in the circle, the energy just seemed to grow and expand. I seemed to get bigger as well. I really enjoyed the tingling feeling it gave me and went back each week to get some more of the magic.

Sometimes I could feel the ancient men around me. I could see them in their fur robes chanting through the night. There was one of them that wore long white robes and had a long white beard. When he raised his hands the energy from the sun, moon and stars filled the whole circle with light. With that kind of energy anything could happen.

Many years ago when people still had stone cottages and wood fires, a great sickness came to this village. Many families died. On that Christmas eve the men of the Macdougell clan came into the ancient circle and sang all night long. They sang ancient songs as well as songs of Christmas. The next day the sickness stopped and the village began to get well and prosper. Every Christmas eve after that night the Macdougells would sing again in the stone circle. They did this every year for two hundred and fifty years. Then their land was taken from them by the Lord of the Manor.

The king had given the land to the Black Lord as a present. The Black Lord made the men work very hard and demanded too many taxes. So they took their families up into the highlands with their sheep and goats. One of the men called Mac was very brave and a descendant from the old Druid wizard. He decided he would change things. That night he had a powerful dream.

The very next Christmas he came back and sang on Christmas eve right in the centre of the circle. The Black Lord of the Manor came to chase him away but behind, Mac the Macdougell, stood all the ghosts of all the previous Macdougells who had sung before. They were dressed in armour. Even the white Druid Wizard was there raising his staff and bringing down the light of the heavens. The Black Lord was terrified and took his family and left that night. The Macdougells returned and have lived here ever since.

Tonight is Christmas eve and the Macdougells have come from far and wide to honour the tradition of singing in the stone circle. The whole village has dressed warmly. We wait gathered together under the full moon and stand close to keep warm. Finally Grandpa Macdougell comes and hums the first note.

We start by singing an old Druid song of the ancient gods. We go on to sing Oh Come All Ye Faithful and many other Christmas carols. We sing until we are warm and our cheeks rosy-red. I can feel the magic spreading far and wide filling everything with light. All my bones feel tingly full. On the hillside just under the moon I can see the ghosts of the ancient Macdougells and Mac himself. We end with the clan song and the ghosts join in as well. Then with warm hearts we go together into the church and have hot drinks and mince pies.

# SKATING

The weather had been very cold and the lake had frozen over. It was the week before Christmas. Everyone was out with their skates. Mr. and Mrs. Pound were skating together waltzing and turning with fancy steps. Little Tom, Sarah and Joe were slipping and sliding and falling down and getting up. It was the first time they had tried the ice and their skates seemed to go everywhere but straight. Little Tom would fall down and then as he got up pulling on Sarah's hand she would fall down. Joe wobbled and somehow managed to stay on his feet. Slowly he came over and taking both Sarah and Tom's hands they all managed to stand up holding each other in a circle. They skated a few steps and then all tumbled down again.

The boys, Rick, Mathew, Greg and George were up to mischief, dashing behind all the girls and putting cold snow down their backs. The girls joined hands and captured one of the boys in the middle and would not let him out. The boys started tossing a snow basketball back and forth until it landed on Mr. Spindle's head. He carefully gathered up the snow and with careful aim sent it straight back.

Elsie was pulling her younger brother and sister on a sledge, all three of them giggling away. They went in and out of the boys poking them whenever they were close enough. The girls gathered around the sledge and helped

Elsie pull it along until they had gone all the way around the lake tickling the boys.

Old Mr. Thomas sat on a log doing up his skates. He was wearing a top hat and as he started to skate he danced a jig and then took the hand of blushing Miss Constance. They were magic to watch as they did figure eights and twists and turns never missing a step. Henry and Susan joined them and soon all four of them were hand in hand skating at a fast and steady pace. They wove in and out of each other and then raced across the lake.

Several cats and dogs decided to try their luck on the ice. They slipped and bounced landing with all four legs going in different directions. At one point the cat jumped into the sledge and took a ride with the two children across the lake. She then scrambled back to the shore. The dogs and cats sat on the side smiling and wagging their tails. Everyone's faces were red and clouds of white breath filled the air. Even the birds were dancing above the crowd adding to the festive afternoon.

Everyone whirled and glided, dancing on the ice. At one point the young and old joined hands and made a chain and wove in and out of one another. They then formed two lines and joined hands and each couple skated through the tunnel of hands. One of the dogs jumped out on the ice and slipped and slid all the way through the two lines. Everyone laughed, clapping.

The large sleigh was brought down and the children were given a ride pulled by the elder boys with brightly coloured ropes. Mr. Thomas had come with his fiddle and everyone danced and sang as they glided along. They skated to waltzes and jigs and Christmas songs. The children in the sleigh gave a chorus of Jingle Bells all on their own. Miss Constance sweetly sang Silent Night. Henry and Susan did all the choruses of We Wish You a Merry Christmas. All too soon the winter sun descended in the west. People changed into their shoes and walked back into the town carrying their skates. The cold lasted and on Christmas day Father Christmas came out to skate giving presents to whoever he met.

# CHOCOLATES

In the middle of a small village there is a shop. It is the most wonderful shop for it is a chocolate shop called Le Bon Chocolat. Here in the kitchen there are great blocks of white chocolate, milk chocolate and deep dark chocolate. There are pans of caramel, nougat, cherries and candies fruits as well as baskets of nuts, brazil nuts, hazel nuts, peanuts, almonds and walnuts. There is thick cream and twelve different kinds of sugar. There are spices of ginger, nutmeg, cinnamon and vanilla. The smell fills the stomach with a yearning for something that is beyond food. This is a shop of heavenly treats and amazing sweet delights.

Here, with great care, squares of caramel are covered with liquid chocolate, cherries are dipped in chocolate like precious jewels and nuts are mixed into small bowls of rich creamy whipped chocolate and placed in moulds of stars and half moons.

At Christmas time each of these hand-made chocolates are decorated with little trees, stars, the head of a smiling Father Christmas or a robin red breast. Almond paste is coloured with berry juices and made into fruits and holly leaves and little animals. There are chocolate logs layered with four kinds of chocolate with a cream centre. There is even a Christmas creche made of almond paste figures in a chocolate stable. The cows and sheep are made of white and dark chocolate and the three kings each carry a box of chocolates for the baby Jesus.

On the shelves there are boxes of mixed chocolates wrapped in bright Christmas paper and special boxes of truffles and brandied fruits. But most of all, the week before Christmas, each child that comes to the shop is able to choose a chocolate out of the basket by the till. Each chocolate is wrapped in special paper with a ribbon for hanging on the tree until Christmas day.

No one is left out at Christmas time at Le Bon Chocolat. They make special boxes for each family from hundreds of chocolates. On Christmas eve Father Christmas himself comes to the shop to gather a surprise for each child of the village. He takes a treat for himself choosing carefully from all the chocolates.

For old Mrs. Rumble there is a box of midnight magic of dark chocolates with cream fillings of white, blue, green and pink. For tiny Tim and his sister there are a bag each of white chocolate stars. Mr. and Mrs. Knight have a fondness for nuts and they have a red box of nut clusters. The Postman, Mr. Williams loves caramel and he will find a postbox filled with different chocolates with caramel centres. Miss Sweetooth will find a chocolate log covered in sugar snow in her stocking on Christmas morning.

This year Le Bon Chocolat has done chocolate animals for all the children of the village. There are giraffes filled with marshmallows and bears with icing fur and elephants with little white chocolate elephants inside. There are chocolate puzzles of robins, owls and christmas trees for the smaller children. The older children have treasure chests filled with sugar coated marbles. For the children who are in hospital the chocolate shop has done a special sugar angel on the top of a Father Christmas box of star shaped chocolates.

At midnight when the three chocolate makers can at last go to sleep, the chocolate itself begins to bubble. It has a smile on its chocolate face as it forms itself into three Christmas bells decorated with a thank-you. These place themselves on the table for the chocolate makers for Christmas day.

# THE SHEEP

It was a cold and frosty night and the innkeeper had put me and the other sheep with the cow and the horse in the stable. We were just munching our hay and oats when two strangers came to where we were. We were used to people staying the night when the inn was full and took no notice of them but went on eating. The lantern gave out a soft light in the stable and there seemed to be a glow coming from the woman. When they had made themselves comfortable on the hay and fed their own donkey, a shepherd came through the door and sat down beside them. He said, 'I have been following a star and it led me to this stable where a heavenly king is to be born.'

The woman smiled. 'Yes, the angels have told me my son will be a son of heaven.' She began to give birth at that moment and before very long there was a new born baby in her arms. There is something wonderful about young babies. Myself and the horse and cow baaed and neighed and mooed to welcome the child to our barn. The baby had the brightest eyes I had ever seen. He smiled at everything. As she suckled him, his head seemed to glow with light.

Then the most amazing thing happened, three kings came through the door. 'We have been following a star and dreamt that a heavenly son would be born here.' Bowing down they gave this shining baby gifts in beautiful boxes. They gave him gold because of the wealth he would bring to the earth and incense for his ability to inspire dreams and myrrh for his precious heart. The baby gave them his warm smile and tears flowed on their faces.

A warm glow filled the stable banishing the winter cold. I felt as if hope was returning to the world. The baby looked at me. I saw a different world. Together, men were harvesting the goodness of the earth. The seas were clear. The forests were full of wild animals. There were no hungry children. Their houses were warm in winter. Everyone lived simply and was happy.

It was like the spirit of spring was returning to the earth when everything blossoms out of the barren winter. This light coming from the child seemed to give hope, sunshine and energy to the world to create food, flowers, new leaves and grass. It warmed my heart and brought a glow to everyone's eyes. Yes, just like my lambs in spring, this baby was giving goodness to everyone around him.

The kings had brought their precious treasures but they were being given the baby's love. The baby was giving all of us the precious gift of bringing a great light into the world. I sighed in contentment and went to sleep watching the baby in his mother's arms.

The next day they continued on their way. I heard later how he had become a great prophet. Ever since that time the stable has had this special light every

Christmas eve. It comes with the night. Slowly a golden glow fills the stable. Then there is a warmth that spreads. Finally I can feel the warmth of his bright smile again and my heart fills with love. It is as though he has come to the stable again. Maybe everywhere he walked has this same beautiful light. The warmth stays with me for the whole year filling me with hope through even the most difficult times.

I am an old sheep now. But I often tell my children of that night. I tell them about the child and how the light came to bless the three kings and the shepherd. I watch as their eyes shine with its wonder and know they too will be blessed with the hope that came that night. May it bless us all.

# THE DRAGON

Ling, the little green dragon, lived in the great cave of the north with his brothers and sisters. The cave had a great green lake which was surrounded in salt sculptures from the dripping water that seeped through the rocks. There were figures of Queens and dancers and horsemen and even a great owl. Ling looked up at the owl and said, 'What is this day called Christmas that the shepherd talks about?' The owl looked at Ling silently and then said, 'Christmas is the day in the year when a god child came to earth. It is his birthday.' 'Does he have a present on his birthday?' asked Ling. 'No, he died a long time ago but everyone still celebrates his birthday. An elf man dressed in red comes and brings the children presents in the night. The children put up their stockings or leave out their shoes and the elf fills them with treats and toys.' 'Do you think he would bring me a present if I left out my rock bowl?' said Ling hopefully. 'You might have to write him a letter to let him know where you live and what you might want,' answered the owl thoughtfully. 'Where does he live?' asked Ling excitedly. 'In the great north under the north star.'

Ling thought to himself for a while and then took out the ancient dragon map of the world. The great north did not look to far away so he thought he would go and visit the Red Elf in person.

He put on his green jumper and woolly hat and packed a lunch of lizards and rock water. He wrote down the directions. Fly over ten large cities and then turn to the left over the great mountain and then fly towards the great north star over the great tundra. With a great swhoosh he flew out of the cave. He flew and he flew until he was hungry and his tummy was rumbling. He landed in the blue mountains filled with heavenly flowers.

A Chinese man came running towards him. 'Oh little dragon I need your help. A wicked creature has stolen the fire of the earth and everywhere is growing colder and colder. You must come with me and relight the cauldron of the earth.' Ling blew some blue fire to warm the man. 'I am on my way to see the Red Elf, but of course I will help you.' The man climbed up Ling's tail and onto his back. They flew to the cave of the Eight Winds.

'Hello,' said the Eight Winds, 'we have been expecting you. We have a fan to give you. If you put it by the fire after it is lit, the fan will keep the fire going at exactly the right temperature. In summer the fire will be blazing hot but in winter it will be only warm.' 'Thank-you,' said Ling. They descended deep into the darkness of the cave.

Suddenly there were two red eyes staring out of the darkness. 'Go away,' said a grumbling old voice, 'I want to keep the fire all to myself so I will be warm in this bitter cold weather.' The little dragon quickly grabbed the creature's ear. 'Ouch, stop it, that hurts,' moaned the creature. The Chinese man held out his torch and Ling breathed fire on it to give them light. There in front of them was a great green toad.

'Listen to me, toad.' 'My name is Gerald,' said the toad. 'Alright Gerald,' said Ling, 'you don't have to keep the fire to warm yourself.' 'What do you mean?' Gerald asked. 'I will relight the fire and then you can sit by it and keep warm all year around. In fact you can be the guardian of the fire if you will promise to look after it.'

And that is what happened. Ling lit the fire and Gerald looked after it. Ling then found the Red Elf who agreed to bring the dragons and Gerald presents for every Christmas after that.

# A CHRISTMAS ROSE

Many years ago there lived a very old lady, in a very old cottage, in a very old wood. She had a beautiful garden with hundreds of flowers. The violets were very shy and only came out when she softly talked to them. The red poppies poked their heads everywhere making her laugh. The harebells hid in the long grass ringing away. The buttercups smiled and sang her their sweet songs. The cow parsley waved its big lacy hands and danced on the breezes. The heather smiled. The lavender's sweet scent perfumed the garden. During the year she would watch to see how each of the wild flower grew. They became very special friends to her. She greeted the violets in the spring with a song. The flowering cherry tree was given a gift of a poem written on a ribbon that would blow in the wind from its branches. She danced around St. John's Wort on the longest day of summer.

When she come into the garden all the flowers opened their blossoms for her. Each day she had a kind word for them and would scatter their seeds far and wide. She gave them delicious drinks of water when the weather was very dry and watched how they would fill themselves up until they could drink no more. She would then sit and drink a lemonade and read them poetry from a very old book covered in velvet. The garden was filled with love.

One day in the afternoon the flowers sat chattering to each other. They decided they would find a way of giving the old woman a special flower. They waited for the moon to come out and watched as the goddess of the garden came down on its moonlight. 'We want to give the old woman a special flower' said the poppy who was never shy of speaking up. 'Yes, it would be nice for her to have a flower in the winter,' said the primrose. All the flowers nodded and smiled at the goddess. 'Well,' she said 'I know of a flower that blossoms in the middle of winter but it lives very far from here. Who could go and get a seed?' 'Whhhooo?' sang the Owl, 'I could be there and back in a night.' 'Thank you owl,' all the flowers said.

Spreading his wings, the Owl flew off into the night. He flew over the town and the mountains. He came to the ocean and flew and flew until he thought the water would never end. He finally came to a land where it was very cold. He took his grey hat out of his pocket and put it over his ears to keep them warm. 'Hello there,' said a white bird. 'Hello,' shivered the Owl. 'Do you know where there is a flower that blooms in winter?' 'Ah you mean the Christmas rose,' said the white bird. 'By the way my name is Will.' 'How do you keep warm?' asked Owl. 'I grow fluff under my feathers,' said Will. 'Come with me and I will show you the roses.'

There in the snow by a mountain spring were the roses

of Christmas. One was white and the other red. 'May I have just one seed of each of you?' asked the Owl. 'Yes, yes!' said the two roses together. Owl flew down and carefully took two of the seeds in his beak. He carefully placed them inside his pocket and flew back across the ocean to the garden.

The flowers were just opening their eyes. 'Oh Owl,' they cried, 'do you have the seeds?' 'Here they are,' he said as he took them out of his pocket. The Goddess planted them in the ground and they blossomed that Christmas and every Christmas after that. The old woman loved them as much as she did all the other flowers. Each Christmas she gathered the seeds and gave them as presents.

# THE PLAY

It was time for the school play. All of the school children were in the room next door and were very excited. The parents had come and were sitting in the hall with the younger brothers and sisters and the granddads and grandmums. The lights dimmed. Slowly everyone went quiet except a little boy who shouted, 'Where is everyone?' Mrs. Hammer began to play the old piano. She went through several tunes, until Miss Softstone waved from the stage. Mrs. Hammer then played a few very loud chords as the older children came on the stage. They sang the Donkey Came to Bethlehem. This they did with great effort and big smiles.

The donkey was in four parts
and each part or person seemed
to bump and trip and tumble
until together they were finally
settled in the stable. They looked
more like a sitting camel than
a donkey. The sheep came in
next singing the Animals Came
to Bethlehem. They scattered
everywhere. The poor shepherd
then had to gather them back
up onto the stage one at a
time. While this was going on
the brave fairy leapt about in
bright pink tights and fluttering
wings, waving a sparkling wand,
singing 'A Miracle, a Miracle'. At
one point, in complete surprise,
she jumped over a sheep who
had lost his way. She paused for
a moment and then leaping over
another sheep in front of her
grinned and said, 'A Miracle.'

It was at this point the little bells came in singing 'Jingle Bells, Jingle Bells, Jingle All the Way.' The little children in the audience sang along. Mrs. Hammer did the song several more times through as everyone had joined in by that time. Her hair was unknotting itself but she kept going without missing a single note.

The sheep were finally settled into a corner waving to their mums and dads. The shepherd was very red faced and finally laid down beside them. At that point, Mary popped up behind the donkey with the baby. The baby was as big as Mary. Joseph said, 'What a fine striking lad he is!' 'Yes,' said Mary, 'he seems to take after his father being so big.'

The very young children arrived dressed as dogs and cats. They each gave the baby a hug and kiss as they walked past. Following them came Tall Tom with a flip chart and a pointer. As he pointed at the words, everyone sang the carols.

Then the three kings arrived singing, 'We Three Kings From Orient are...' They gave their presents to the baby who opened each one with great joy and a loud ripping of paper. The baby then hugged each of the kings knocking off a crown or two. The entire school was now on stage singing, 'We wish you a Merry Christmas and a Happy New Year.' The fairy then waved her wand and wished everyone a Merry Christmas and a joyous holiday as she rode on a sheep.

The children all bowed and the parents and grandparents clapped and clapped until every one had to sing Jingle Bells all over again. Then real jingle bells could be heard from outside the room. With a 'ho ho ho', Father Christmas appeared with a wheelbarrow full of presents. Lucy exclaimed, 'Why does he have on my dad's boots?' This was ignored. All the children's names were called out one by one as they received a present.

They were soon unwrapping their surprises. The teachers smiled and all the children abandoned themselves to their parents. There were drinks and cakes to calm everyone down. Slowly the sheep, angels, kings and others walked home for the festive holidays.

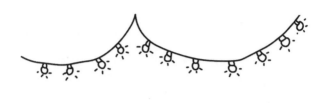

# TEDDY

Mary had never made a stuffed toy before but had always wanted to make a bear. She went to the shop and bought a pattern and some material and some soft stuffing. She found some old buttons and bright red cloth for the nose and mouth and ears and feet. She pinned and stitched and finally stuffed the teddy. She then made him a waistcoat with a little red pocket and a hat with holes for his ears.

The Teddy then winked. Mary rubbed her eyes and the Teddy winked again. 'Did you just wink?' she asked. The Teddy winked again and smiled. She smiled back wondering if she had just fallen into a dream and would wake up soon. The Teddy got up and bounced into her lap. Feeling a bit foolish she said, 'Would you like a bounce or just a cuddle?' The Teddy smiled and said, 'Both please.' As she cuddled him and bounced him, she said, 'Do you talk to everyone?' 'I don't know as I have just been made, but I feel deep down in my stuffing it would be nice to have someone to talk to. I think teddies are meant to talk to the people they are with. I love secrets too.' 'My goodness!' said Mary, 'I will have to find you a special friend.' 'Yes,' said Teddy, 'Someone young like me to play with.'

Mary thought to herself and then just the person came to mind. 'Would you mind if I wrapped you up for Oscar?' 'Who is Oscar?' 'He is a little

boy in the hospital I work in.'
'Sounds perfect to me.' So
Mary wrapped Teddy in Father
Christmas paper and took him
to the hospital. She put a bright
red card on the parcel with
Oscar's name.

It was the afternoon Father
Christmas came to the hospital
to give all the children a present
as they sat under the tree. Father
Christmas arrived with his big
sack. The children sang him
several Christmas songs. One
little girl read him a poem she
had written. Another little boy
sang him a song. Then all the
children performed a short play
about the Owl who gave all
the forest animals presents for
Christmas. When this was over
the children sat around the tree
in the corner of the hospital

ward. Some were on crutches and others in wheel chairs and others in beds. They all waited as Father Christmas gave them each a present.

When Oscar opened his present he was a bit disappointed as he had hoped for a car or even a gameboy. But then Teddy winked at him and Oscar winked back. Then Teddy said 'How old are you?' 'About eight, but how come you can talk?' 'How come you can talk?' 'Well people are suppose to talk not stuffed bears!' 'Well this bear talks but not to everyone so it is just as well we are alone at the moment!'

Oscar told Teddy about his operation and showed him his scar. 'That must have hurt.' said Teddy. 'No, not really because they put you to sleep,' said

Oscar. 'Do they feed you well in this place?' asked Teddy. 'It is okay but I would really like some good chips.'

Teddy quietly tiptoed out of the hospital down to the chip shop. 'Hello,' he smiled at the lady making the chips. 'I would like some chips for my friend Oscar.' 'Would you like salt and vinegar on them?' she asked thinking he was a small kid dressed as a bear. 'That would be just perfect,' said Teddy. He came back with the chips wrapped in paper with salt and vinegar carrying a package of ketchup. Oscar ate every last one. 'That was delicious.' 'Anything for you,' said Teddy. Oscar and Teddy became great friends and only Mary ever knew their secret.

# A FATHER
# CHRISTMAS
# PRESENT

Little Timothy Manner was lying in his bed before going to sleep thinking about Christmas. He was six years old but often thought about things before going to sleep. He knew Father Christmas came in the night with hundreds of presents for children all over the world. But, thought Timothy, who brought Father Christmas a present? He thought and he thought and then he remembered that his Gran and Mum and Dad gave each other presents. Yes, it was too much to do if Father Christmas had to give to everyone. So he must only give to the children. In that case, who gave Father Christmas his present, he thought to himself before drifting off to sleep.

He dreamt he was in the house of Father Christmas. There were empty coffee cups and papers and lists and half eaten sandwiches and no tree or decorations. Father Christmas was working hard in his garage wrapping present after present. 'Excuse me,' said Timothy, 'but what would you like for Christmas?' He looked up not at all surprised to see a small boy standing next to him and said, 'I would really like some warm stocks and some good books to read by the fire.'

When Timothy woke up he raced down the stairs picking up Fluff his cat on the way. 'Oh, Fluff, we must get Father

Christmas a present.' He opened the kitchen door and shouted, 'We must do something about Father Christmas not having a present!' His Mum and Dad looked at their son with amazement as he continued, 'No it is true, we must give Father Christmas a present. I dreamt he was all alone and too busy to get himself something. He said he would like some warm socks and some good books. It isn't fair. We must do something about it.' 'Slow down Timothy,' said his Dad, 'and explain what you are talking about.' 'I dreamt about Father Christmas and he needs us to come and give him a present. Please can we go?'

So they found out where Father Christmas lived. They put on their warm clothes and took a plane to Iceland. There they met an Eskimo and went with him on his sleigh pulled by eight husky dogs. They traveled over drifts and drifts of snow and up mountains and down valleys until at last they came to the house of Father Christmas.

When they knocked at the door a snowman came out. He said, 'Father Christmas left a few hours ago.' 'Oh good,' said Timothy, 'we have come to give him a surprise for Christmas. Can we come in?' 'Of course,' smiled the snowman, 'I will help you.' They set to work and cleaned and tidied his house. They decorated the tree and put a turkey in the oven and left him a Christmas cake and three parcels wrapped in Father Christmas paper.

They bundled themselves up in the sleigh and caught the last plane and arrived home just in time for Christmas eve. They were tired but decorated their tree and put the presents out for the next day. Timothy hung up his stocking thinking of the surprise Father Christmas was going to have.

The next day the phone rang and it was Father Christmas. 'Timothy my little friend,' said Father Christmas, 'thank you for making my Christmas the best ever! I really like the bright red jumper, the books, the woolly socks, your picture and the chocolate selection.' 'You are welcome,' said Timothy with a smile, 'and thank you for mine. The building set was just what I wanted.'

# THE STAR

There was a deep frost in the night and the sky was brilliantly clear. So clear, that every star seemed like a tiny diamond sparkling over the still, calm earth. The sheep and the goats were nestled together in the barn. Jill gave them their hay and patted each one on the head. She then came out of the barn and looked at the stars overhead. There was Orion with his bow, the Big Dipper with the North Star and Venus on the horizon. The Milky Way was full of white mist and thousands of stars. As she scanned the sky, she felt the presence of the great star spirit beasts, the ram, the scorpion, the bull and others. Then she noticed a very bright star near the planet

Jupiter. It twinkled and winked and was full of rainbow colours.

Suddenly the star dropped down from the sky and stood by her side. 'Who are you?' she asked with delight never having seen a beautiful star being before. 'Oh, I am the star of the silver mountains,' it said smiling. 'And where are they?' asked Jill. The star chuckled a twinkling star laugh and said, 'They are the mountains deep in the darkness of the sky where the great spirits live. They have asked me to come to take you there for a visit.'

She took the star's hand and they flew up into the dark sky, past whirling stars and red giants and black holes and white dwarfs until they came to a beautiful country filled with blue fountains and magic flowers and wise smiling ancient men and women. Jill had tea with the Great Empress. She was dressed in green jade and said, 'Tell me about earth.' 'Well,' said Jill, 'where I live there are lots of green fields and the animals are happy. But nearby there is a city where everyone looks grey and unhappy. The air is cloudy with grey-fumes and the water tastes like metal. The only place in the city that is good are the parks and the rivers. When I am in the park I can breath again.' 'Well,' said the Great Empress, 'We will have to do something about that.'

She clapped her hands and called Lu and Ku. 'Lu, go and get your great broom and take it down to the city and sweep the air clean. Ku, you go and get the great river and rain and wash the city.' 'Yes, your Empress,' they smiled, 'we will go to work at once.' Lu took his broom and Ku his river and bucket and off they went whistling away.

Suddenly a great storm filled the city with wind and water until the city was completely clean and shiny again. 'Wow,' exclaimed Jill, 'Now everything will be sparkling bright for Christmas.' She and the Great Empress then ate peaches and cakes and drank more green tea. 'Now', said the Great Empress, 'What would you like for Christmas? I am allowed to give you one wish.' Jill sipped her green tea and thought carefully. Then she smiled and said shyly, 'It would be nice if all the animals could have twins this year. Then no young animal would be on its own.' 'That is a very good wish,' said the Great Empress, 'so be it.' Lao Tzu came to the garden and presented Jill with a little jade statue of the Buddha. 'Just rub his tummy when you are in difficulty and he will help,' Lao Tzu said kindly.

The star came and they flew back to earth. Jill found herself staring at the sky and the great star twinkling overhead. She looked at the little Buddha in her hand and safely put him in her pocket for when she might need him. 'Thank you,' she said to the night stars, 'that is the best Christmas present ever.' She went inside to the warm fire and the sleeping cat by the stove and made a cup of tea and cut a piece of Christmas cake.

# CHRISTMAS EVE

At last it was Christmas eve. The tree was standing by the fireplace and all the boxes of decorations were on the rug. Dad had put up the ladder and was hanging strings of gold, silver, red and green beads. Mum was sorting out the coloured glass bulbs, each one from a different year and from a different shop. Some had stars on them, and others had Father Christmas or robins or snow flakes. Each one was very special and very different. There were big angels and small angels and even old fashion angels. Kit and Sally were making toy figures and animals to hang on the lower branches. Finally Dad put the great star on the top.

The tree was soon covered with streams of beads, coloured bulbs, animals of all descriptions and small carefully wrapped surprises. Mum clipped on the holders for the candles and placed a small white candle in each one. When everything had at last had been placed on the tree, they turned off the lights and lit the candles one by one. It was always a beautiful moment when the tree lit up with dancing candle light. They each had a glass of warm apple cider and toasted the tree and Christmas eve.

Kit hung up his stocking that was striped in red and white from the toe to the top. Sally placed hers next to his on the chimney. Hers was all red with white fur at the top. Together they put the biscuits they had made on a Christmas plate next to a glass of sherry and a note for Father Christmas. They had drawn their own special pictures to thank him for what he might bring them in the night.

Dad lit the fire in the fireplace while Mum went into the kitchen and made hot drinks and brought them out on a large tray with sandwiches and cakes. They all ate, enjoying the tree glimmering in the dark. 'I think this is the most wonderful tree in the world.' laughed Sally. Kit then sang While Shepherds Watched. They sat together and watched the fire dance. Dad read them a Christmas Tale by Charles Dickens. It was about an Old Scrooge who would not celebrate Christmas. So one

Christmas eve the three ghosts of Christmas past, present and future came to visit in the night. Old Scrooge realized all that he was missing and how he could bring happiness to his family. 'I just love Tiny Tim in that story,' sighed Sally.

When everything was tidied up, the children gathered the presents they had secretly wrapped from under their beds and placed the brightly wrapped parcels under the tree. Mum was still hanging chocolates and other small presents on the branches. Dad had opened the box of presents from Uncle Tim in Australia and arranged them under the tree. 'The tree looks so beautiful.' said Sally. 'Can we stand around it and hold hands?' When they had done that she said, 'I wish that all the children of the world will have presents on Christmas Day.' They held hands and wished together with their eyes closed. High in the heavens the angels smiled. Finally with sleepy heads and long yawns they went to bed to dream of what Christmas day might bring.

At midnight there was the soft sound of sleigh bells and a rustle as Father Christmas slid down the chimney and filled the stockings from tip to toe with the most wonderful things. He drank the sherry, ate the biscuits and admired the pictures. He put his bag over his shoulder and with a leap rose up the chimney. In his sleigh, giving a wink he quietly said, 'Merry Christmas to all and to all a good night.'

## YOUR CHRISTMAS PICTURE

# YOUR CHRISTMAS STORY

## ABOUT THE AUTHOR

Each night before going to sleep I would write on odd bits of paper left over from my grandfather's printing works. I always seemed to have a pen in hand. When I went to school I would quickly finish my work and then write stories on school paper. I was probably the only child who read every book in the school library. I would often leave bits of paper in the books about further adventures the characters could have. One day I decided that other people might like to read my stories. So I started to print books just like my grandfather. He used a hand printing press while I use a computer. This Christmas I wrote stories about my favourite characters. Next Christmas I will write about all my favourite trees. I hope children young and old will enjoy them.

**DEBRA KAATZ**

# ABOUT THE ILLUSTRATOR

I have enjoyed drawing for as long as I can remember. As children my sister and I would spend hours drawing greetings cards for any special or made up occasion. We made little books and comics to sell to our neighbours for 10p. Later I went to Art College where I learned more about illustration. I also studied animation, making short films using puppets and tiny props and scenery which I built myself. I have been lucky enough to end up doing a job that I enjoy. Each piece of work presents a new challenge. I love being able to start with a blank sheet of paper and fill it with thoughts and ideas. Now I have a one-year-old daughter, who already loves her books. I hope she will continue to find stories and pictures as endlessly fascinating as I have done.

EMILY SKINNER

## YOUR CHRISTMAS WISH